Jan Laurens Siesling

How the Rhino Lost its Horn

&

Other Just So Songs

JUST SO **J!S** EDITIONS

I wrote this little cycle of verse for young people immediately after reading *POACHED: Inside the Dark World of Wildlife Trafficking,* an eye-opening exploration of the thoroughly saddening & maddening massacre of the world's animals. The book is written by science journalist Rachel Nuwer, published by Da Capo Press, New York, 2018. More people should know it and see that all I tell in these pages is true too. I thought that perhaps young people, after enjoying an honest little story in rhyme, would convince old people to buy and read *POACHED.* The other way round is fine, too.

ISBN 978-1-0878-1488-9

In the year of Greta Thunberg

to my daughter Yolanda

to my grandsons Swann, Orlando, Sami and Ulysse

Table of Contents

I.

How the Rhinoceros Lost its Horn

1.

One Rhino there was in Uganda,

Her horn was found in a Honda,

From her nose it was sawn,

Between night and dawn,

Now no Rhino there is in Uganda.

2.

One Rhino there was in Zimbabwe,

She was lying not far from the Parkway.

Her legs in the air,

Her horn was not there,

It was on its way to Vientiane.

3.

One Rhino there was in the Congo,

She was white, this is long ago,

She was killed for her horn

Before her baby was born

And buried with her in utero.

4.

One Rhino there was in Angola,

And she did not die of Ebola.

She was luckier than the man,

Who poached her for 1000 Yuan.

She was black and her horn is in China.

5.

One Rhino there was in the country of Chad

She lost her horn and was sadder than sad

I look like a dinosaur, she said,

In the year of the meteor, she said,

An extinct species before even I'm dead.

6.

One last Rhino, named Sudan in Sudan,

Was kidnapped and brought to a zoo then.

He took a plane many times in his life,

With his sperm and his horn and his wife,

And died of old age not so far from South-Sudan.

7.

No rhinos now live in Great Africa,

They're rooted out like in Europa.

After the ice age as before

Man wages a cruel war

On his most peaceful flora and fauna.

II.

How the Elephant lost its Tusks

In the middle of Mother Africa

Happened a little drama,

When a kid-phant in the savanna

Strolled with his elephant mama.

His daddy was far and so was his aunt

And his uncle was at the water pond.

But close stood a man with a shining gun,

The gun had even spectacles on.

That gun could not miss such a big mom.

It shot also the kid — for the fun,

Because a gun is a gun is a gun.

And the toddler-phant didn't run — from his mom.

Already the vultures hovered in the air,

It smelled blood, sweat and tears over there.

For the ivory tusks the birds did not care,

That was the gunman's unique affair.

Then the father cried, and uncle, and aunt,

At the breast of Mother Africa.

Too late the world heard them lament.

The kid was the last of the continent.

III.

How the Pangolin Lost its Scales

Why oh why

is the pangolin shy?

When I try

To get close by?

Why oh why

does the pangolin roll

like a ball

when I troll

it and call

it … my panacea?

19

Let us stop whying now

The pangolins are dying now.

Why?

Because of fools like you … and I.

Well, look at the scales,

Aren't they miraculous like fairy tales?

They sure can cure cancer, you see it from here,

If you mix them in your beer.

They whiten your teeth and brighten your breath

If you add toothpaste on your brush

They flatten hunchbacks, which is not the same

As arching flatfoot, that universal shame.

Your hair will not turn gray

If you swallow one every day.

Your blood will not turn blue

If you put some in your shoe.

Believe it or not, but you better try,

It must be true since we don't know why.

Oh wonderful pangolin scales,

Better than … my fingernails!

Grandmother heard it

From her grandmother's granny. Wow!

Grand-granny's aunt observed it

In her fourth husband, who doubts now?

He drank pangolin wine, a liter a day,

He lived, the other three died, okay?

The Purple Emperor wrote on stones

That pangolin scales revived old bones

So his concubine made soup of them,

Or soap, it's unclear, but a bathtub full.

Now everyone sees purple or pimp

And thinks of himself as Emp or Imp.

Which makes that the innocent pangolins

Are killed by those cruelest hobgoblins,

Hundreds per day, thousands per week…

It's their own fault, they are so weak,

Can't even survive the blade of an axe

Or bullets in their necks and backs!

We fools are too many and they are too rare,

They are lovely, but we do not care.

Unfortunately, only one thing is sure,

Do not call this a sinecure:

Pangolin flesh, blood and scales, perhaps

Heal maladies and other mishaps,

Beat toothache and the plague bacillus,

Warts on the nose and peccadillos,

Fear of spiders and the smallpox,

Pimples on the butt and on the rocks,

Schizophrenia and kleptomania,

Agoraphobia, what more, hypochondria …

Apparently, however,

Evil hearts they cure never.

While soothing so many pains,

They do not ever heal sick brains.

IV.

The Ballad of the Whale

Son, tell your son:

"There were whales in the seas,

There were whales in the oceans,

When my father was a son like you."

Son, tell your son:

"There was a whale in the sea,

There was a whale in the ocean,

When I was a son like you."

Son, tell your son:

"There are no whales in the seas,

There is no whale in the ocean,

Now you are my son."

Your son will say: "Dad,

Where did the whales go from the sea,

Where did the whales go from the ocean,

When your father was a son like me?"

Your son will say: "Dad,

Where did the whale go from the sea,

Where did the whale go from the ocean,

When you were a son like me?"

Your son will say: "Dad,

Why are there no whales in the sea,

Why is there no whale in the ocean,

Now I am your son?"

Son, you will say, "Son,

The whales went into ships on the sea

The whales went into ships on the ocean,

To be skinned and be boned."

Son, you will say: "Son,

The whales went into restaurants,

The whales went into pots and pans

They went into tins and cans."

Son, you will say: "Son,

The whales were eaten up by men,

The whales were eaten up by sons.

Now in the oceans there are none."

V.

I Loved the Tiger

I loved the tiger

And the tiger loved me

I was a boy

And he protected me

He would meet me in the suite

Of my blanket and my sheet

In the secret of the night

He would turn off all the lights

How warm it was and sure

The thieves stayed at the door

I was the only one to see

That the tiger was with me

I made myself so very small
I rolled myself into a ball
I curled myself into the nest
Between his arms for endless rest

He eyed me with his tiger eyes
He licked me with his tiger tongue
He kissed me with his tiger lips
He tickled me close to my hips

His fur his muscles and his tail
His whiskers teeth nail after nail
I stroked them with my little hand
His body was my promised land

From him I learned what beauty is
For me his strength was tenderness
From him I learned desire
I was his friend and he my sire

He was the image of the lord
He was the scepter and the sword
I told the devil go to hell
I cast on him my tiger spell

I loved the tiger
And the tiger loved me
Today I am old but where is he
I heard he is in agony

I heard the tiger's flesh and bones
Are served in porcelain terrines
His claws and teeth in powder form
A substitute for aspirins

I heard his blood is boiled and
Drunk by men weaker than worms
His noble manhood broiled and
Chewed by men lower than germs

I heard he was extinct in China
Exterminated in Siberia
Hunted down in holy India
And farmed as a cow in Southeast-Asia

My lord! You are crucified and gone

To hell and the devil has won

And I have lost both you and me

O lord! how would I have died for thee!

VI.

Black Bear Bile

Once upon a time, there was a bear

In the country of the Khmer.

Or was it the country of the Viet?

Yes, dear old country of the Viet!

The bear was big, his name was Black. It

Was the color of his jacket.

Had he a white stain on his nose?

Yes, Black had a white stain on his nose.

Strolling on all fours, he seemed small,

Standing on his hind feet, he was tall.

Taller than the tallest man,

Yes, taller than the tallest woman.

Black must have been, so you suppose,

King of the jungle, King Whitenose,

Strong and gentle, just and feared,

Yes, strong but gentle, just but feared.

He must have loved, you're right to think,

Honey and berries, acorns and pink

Salmon, straight from the creek,

Yes, silver salmon from the icy creek.

You hope he's married a good wife

And has kids, maybe four or five,

And leads a black bear family life,

Yes, a jolly black bear family life.

But no, not the forest, but a farm

Is black bear's home, and a barn

Is black bear's house, and a cage

Is his room, yes, a little iron cage

Made of iron bars, with no wood floor,

And this windy room has no door

To come out, a prison it really is,

Yes, an iron prison it really is.

On his hind legs he never stands,

All his life he sits on his hands

Bread and water is his daily meal,

Yes, old bread, dirty water, his meal.

Black never committed a crime,

But was imprisoned for a lifetime;

A cub, he was, stolen from his mom,

Yes, a cub, stolen from his sorry mom.

A hole was drilled through his black bear skin

Down to his liver with a tube and a pin.

I don't know how they could get it in,

No, don't want to know how they got it in

To suck his bile every Sunday night,

With blood and pus mixed in all right.

How I would cry, if it were me

Yes, how I'd cry, if it were poor me.

On Monday morn Black's bile is sold

To a doctor or a quack or an old

or sick or dumb individual,

Yes, a dumb sick old living soul.

Now you think that I invent-

ed this horror story of one cent.

No alas! Every word is true to life.

Yes alas! Each word is true to life.

You wonder how a human soul

Can be so cruel, stupid and so foul,

To kill a bear during twenty years,

Yes, kill a bear for twenty bloody years.

VII.

Armadillo Road Star

Who has never seen

Armadillo in the real

Has never been riding

In an automobile.

Describe Armadillo:

A North-American

Solitary dead mammal

Lying at the roadside.

His feet point to the sky,

Or are they hers?

How to tell from a car

At sixty-five mph?

Looking out of the right window

You can see it very well

During two seconds

And a half or three.

Mother says: so many!

Soon none will be left.

Father says: so many!

The woods are overflowing.

Armadillo is always alone

Because no father, no mother,

No kid or cat ever halts

And says: hi! How are y'all doing?

So alone, it would like to weep

But cannot do that still,

So sad, it would like to vanish

From our eyes and, no doubt, it will.

VIII.

Fish Boys and Fish Girls

Little fish boys went to school
With the fish girls in the pool
The master was so big and strong
That what he said was never wrong

He had a book that was very old
But every page was full he told
With many plates and letters too
A little watery but true

The book was called ecology
And no one knew what that could be
The master said it was history
Of the ocean and the sea

One day said he they would take a bus

One big enough for the whole good class

And ride to the far end of the pool

And even further wasn't it … cool

And from the edge they would observe

The master used such a difficult verb

The desert that was newly made

For the wedding of technique and trade

A desert the fish boys had never seen

In it the fish girls had never been

Sir Technique must be a Terminator

Lady Trade a giant Alligator

Finally it was the final day the bus

Was big enough for the whole good class

And the master too he drove so fast

The fish kids would see a desert at last

And from the border of the border

Standing on tiptail in good order

Fish boys and fish girls watched the water

And saw nothing nothing but … water

As far as their fishy eyes could see

Nothing but water in the endless sea

Nothing but water in the ocean blue

Just like the swimming pool in the zoo

No handsome heroes in tiny suits

No mermaids with their tiny ~~boobs~~ boots

No alligators or crocodiles

With crocodile tears or crocodile smiles

Such is the desert so spoke the teacher

When it comes to the ocean no creature

Can live here too hot it is too dry

For a spider or a fish or a fly

Like a white washing machine

The sea now is empty and clean

Apart from the plastic and the oil

On its surface and in its soil

Look there! cried in choir the kids, Master!

There comes a sea monster! where?

It was a boat with electric nets

It caught all the fish in one last catch

IX.

Something Went Wrong

O my beloved and wonderful creature

I must tell you a tale

Before you lie down, it is late

And you must listen

O truly beloved creature

Your race is a terrible race

I created the earth for you

And created you for the earth

I invented life for you

And you for life

I am still proud of myself

Said with sincere modesty

It was quite a success
If one compares it to other blind shots
In the endless darkness
Boring and so repetitive

Life made all the difference
I needed indeed a few billion years
To find the right combination
But you do look like your maker

Just as fine as I imagined you
At my tentative beginnings
But after all a billion years feel
Not so different from a million

Don't be surprised that I love you

Every one of you apart

Every one of you born as an infant

Everyone loved loving and lovable

O naive and surprising creature

Where did it go wrong

Where did I go wrong

Where did we … arm in arm go wrong

Something did go wrong

Something worth a billion years

Of hard work and deep hope

But your race is a terrible race

I had made the rose for you and

The eagle and the fox so bright

And honey and the secret of the woods

And the moon to kiss you in the night

Something went wrong

You want to leave our earth

Focus of your greatest brains

Anguish of your united intelligence

You want more than dolphins

In transparent oceans more

Than dragonflies over the creek

More than the return of spring

You look for life out there

Where there is none but

A void of a billion years

No voice resounds in the silence

In your dream you call for Venus

Mars and Mercury the moons

Of Saturn but Saturn you remember

Devoured his children like stones

O my tender and smart kid

I know you since I made you

And forgive you all your flaws

Life searches life what else

Such was my bet (I smile)

From the hesitant beginnings

Life searches life and

You call love one of my names

I gave you the rivers and the fish

I gave you the air and the birds

I gave you the prairies and the beasts

I gave you the flowers and the fruits

I gave you the life you search

I gave you the love you need

I gave you a baby in your arms

I gave you beauty in your eyes

Something went wrong

O my beloved and infinitely dear

O my beloved and unbelievably wicked

You look for life out there

But you kill the life out here

You kill the bears and the bees

You kill the tigers and the trees

You kill the chimpanzees

You kill the lice and the fleas

You kill the whales in the seas

You kill the penguins and the tuna

And the lion and the puma

And the coral in the coral sea

All the life I gave thee

O my bewitched, as an adieu

Will you then also kill me?

You clean the earth so thoroughly

You wipe the good with the bad

Soon it will look more like a moon

You also will be gone

For another billion years

Which will feel like a trillion

A trillion years to cry my tears

And wonder what went wrong

X.

Your Hand is My Hand

Two children I saw walking on a shore
The sun was setting amidst red clouds
How old they were I couldn't tell
They were alone and I felt unwell

I was holding on my father's pants
The sea was whispering and the wind
Blew freely in the golden sand
The beach was empty from end to end

When I first saw them they were far
And tinier than butterflies
My eyes were fixed on them and feared
For them until they disappeared

Struggling firm against the breeze
Smaller again than the smallest birds
Barefoot and never looking up they went
As far as could be on the humid strand

They had no parents they had no friends
I puzzled my wits on father's bike
My arms around his biking waist
The clouds now gathering in haste

Beyond the horizon of my mind
Two children were walking on and on
Until they arrived into my dreams
I've loved them all my life it seems

A girl they were and a boy alone
Between the sea the sand and the sun
But this do not forget my friend
They walked together hand-in-hand

To the very end

Come said the Muse,

Sing me a song no poet has yet chanted,

...

(Walt Whitman)